JUDE'S BEST
Worst Day Ever

Catherine Clark Felts

Illustrated by Carla and James Ramos

To request permission, contact the publisher at:
　　　publisher@innerpeacepress.com

ISBN: 978-1-958150-40-5
Jude's Best Worst Day Ever

First publication: November 2024

Published by **Inner Peace Press**
Eau Claire, Wisconsin, USA
www.innerpeacepress.com

For Cate and Cassie, the two beats of my heart,
and Colin, my biggest supporter and greatest love.

For Heather, for taking a chance on fate.

Jude sighed every few moments,
pushing his eggs around his plate.

"Today is the WORST day ever!" Jude groaned.

"Oh darling, there will be a lot of worst days ever," Jude's mother said. "You and Buddy have until the sun starts to set. See if you can make your last day with Buddy the BEST worst day ever."

Jude jumped down and ran out onto the porch.
The screen door banged and Buddy stirred.
His gray whiskers snuffled, his sore bones
creaked as he stretched.

"C'mon, Buddy! Let's go. We're gonna find a
way to have the best BEST day ever!" Jude said
as he bounded into the grass.

Buddy struggled to follow. Jude had heard about a way to make wishes come true and was desperate to try it. He gulped air, held it for a count of twenty, twirled around three times, jumped on one foot seven times, and nearly fell shouting to the universe:

"I WISH BUDDY WAS A PUPPY AGAIN!"

Jude's jaw dropped open as Buddy was instantly a puppy. His gray whiskers gone, replaced with coal black, he was bouncing up and down with puppy energy.

Giddy and out of breath, Jude tried a second wish. Another gulp of air held for twenty seconds, three twirls, seven jumps on one foot, and Jude fell down as he shouted to the universe:

"I WISH I WAS A PUPPY!"

A few moments later, Jude tried standing on two legs but found it more comfortable to stand on four. He scratched behind his ear with his foot.

When he opened his mouth to talk, his tongue fell
out three inches too far. Jude ran circles around
Buddy, with his new tail wagging hard enough
to blow dandelion fluffs into the air.

Jude and Buddy dashed down to the stream and splashed around in the cool, crisp water. They watched fish swimming up stream, but couldn't quite catch them in their slobbering jowls.

Years ago, during their first summer together, they had watched tadpoles dart about and threw leaves into the stream to see how quick the flow was each day.

APPALACHIAN TRAIL

As the sun rose higher, Buddy shook the cool water off and headed back to the porch. Jude followed. Jude helped himself to the PB&J sandwich set out by his mother. Buddy chomped down the special treat of ground steak in his bowl. It reminded Jude of Buddy's birthdays,, a grand celebration with an entire juicy steak.

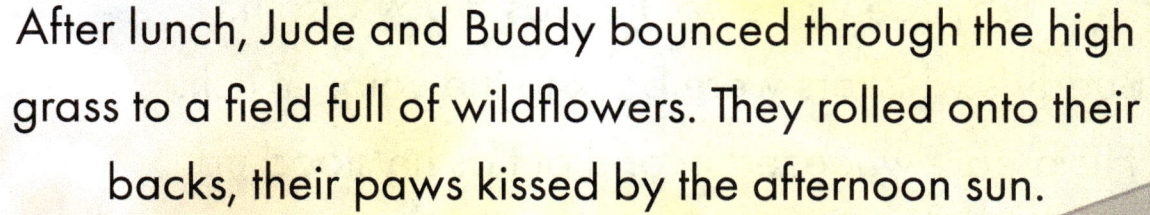

After lunch, Jude and Buddy bounced through the high grass to a field full of wildflowers. They rolled onto their backs, their paws kissed by the afternoon sun.

This was their favorite spot, where they had played and snoozed through each spring, summer, and fall. As the heat rose, they slipped into a nap.

When Jude woke up, he was a boy again.
Buddy's whiskers were back to the color of ash.
His breath wheezed in and out as he stood up.

With the sun moments away from setting, Jude
ran back to his mother and exclaimed "I did it!
I found a way to make this the best BEST day ever!
I can make wishes come true!"

Buddy struggled up the steps,
tuckered out from trying to keep up.

"Darling, I'm so happy for you. Wishes do come true, sometimes. I know you had the best day you could." Jude's mom scratched Buddy's ear.

"Just wait and see," Jude said. He swallowed air and held it, twirled, hopped, and yelled out:

"I WISH BUDDY DIDN'T HAVE TO GO!"

Jude's mother hugged him. "I wish he didn't have to go, too. But we can help Buddy in the best possible way. He wouldn't want anyone else but you there to comfort him."

Picking up Buddy with care, she placed him on a bed of blankets in the back of the pickup. Then she and Jude got into the cab. They drove down the long winding dirt driveway, heading to the vet.

The sun set. The crickets were singing their evening symphony as the old pickup crunched back up the driveway. Jude ran into the house with Buddy's blue collar in his hand.

As the days passed, some were harder than others. The first time Jude smiled was when he donated Buddy's toys, unused food, and washed blankets to the shelter. He knew that they would go to help someone else's best friend. It took some time, but Jude stopped reaching for the familiar soft fur under the table.

After thinking carefully, Jude placed Buddy's
ashes on the table in the family room. Every late
afternoon, the sun would kiss Buddy's paws. Jude
knew they could both feel the warmth of the sun,
reminding them of the best worst day ever.

ADULT GUIDEBOOK

As we transition to the Adult Guidebook, I'd like to inform you I'm not an educated expert on grief and loss. I have no formal education on the topic, have no degrees, no certificates. However, I am human. I am a caring and compassionate mother of two amazing little girls and I have experienced loss before. When I was in my twenties, I worked at an animal shelter. This shelter had a policy that animals were never euthanized because of lack of space or because they had been in the shelter for a long time. Regardless, we occasionally made the best decision for the animals to euthanize to relieve their pain. I held the paw and stared into the eyes of numerous shelter animals as they were given relief and euthanized. I wanted them to know they weren't alone and someone loved them in their last moments. I have lost my own family pets as a child and as an adult. The loss, the pain, the grief is a shared experience felt by all who have had to say goodbye to cherished animals. I encourage you to seek additional help as needed and utilize the resources and discussion topics included in this guide as you navigate through the journey of loss.

Grief and loss affect everyone, but it's important to understand that children may not always express their emotions outwardly or in a way that is easy to identify as caregivers. Understanding and supporting children through their grief is crucial, though it can be challenging to navigate and find the best approaches for the child.

Children may not show their grief openly. Their reactions can be internal and hard to articulate. Children, similar to adults, experience grief through various stages. Their responses to loss can be inconsistent and may include regression in behavior. Young children may not grasp the permanence of death, while older children might have more complex questions.

There are many ways to support a grieving child. It's important to normalize and validate feelings. Talk about grief using simple language, sharing your own feelings of sadness.

Children and caregivers can honor the loss of a pet by performing activities like those listed below. These activities also provide an opportunity and environment to openly discuss feelings and concerns about death and loss.

Create a memorial display. Decorate a photo frame that will hold a cherished picture of your pet.

Create a scrapbook using stickers, crayons, markers, glue, construction paper, and other art supplies to honor the memories with your pet.

Write a story, song, book, or poem about your pet.

Write a letter to your pet.

Donate supplies, money, or time to a local animal shelter.

Plant a tree, flower, or garden in memory of your pet.

Create a memorial video honoring the memories of your pet using sections of previous recordings. Add music or a spoken message, like a poem.

Create an outdoor memorial for your pet in your yard or garden.

Donate toys at a dog park along with a photo and message about your pet, so everyone who uses the toys can share in the remembrance of your pet.

Visit www.CatherineClarkFelts.com to download a free activity sheet that contains step-by-step instructions on how to create a Scrapbook Page honoring your cherished pet.

To help initiate the conversation with your child, here are some questions to ask and discuss:

What did your pet enjoy most?

What do you miss most about your pet?

How would you like to honor your pet?

What activity can we do together?

What was your best day with your pet?

What is the hardest part of loss?

How does it make you feel?

How did you spend time with your pet?

Be honest and truthful about death and provide clear explanations. Provide consistent support by maintaining routine. Be patient and gentle, allowing space for the child's emotions. Encourage expression using creative outlets, like drawing, writing or other activities to help the child express their feelings. Create remembrance opportunities and find ways to remember the deceased, such as sharing stories or participating in memorial activities. Seek additional resources like support groups, professional counseling, or faith-based support. Below are resources that offer additional information on how to support a child through grief.

National Alliance for Children's Grief: https://nacg.org
Children's Bereavement Center: https://childbereavement.org/
Winston's Wish: https://winstonswish.org/
Rainbows Bridge: https://www.rainbowsbridge.com/

Above all, grant yourself grace and patience as you provide love, support, compassion, and validation to the child.

About the Author

Catherine Clark Felts lives in Chester, Virginia, with her three mischievous cats, two amazing daughters, and one loving and supportive husband. An avid runner, she finds the best time to mull over a book concept is during an early morning jog. Formerly a technical support team Director and degreed Bioprocess Engineer, she felt the call to write and continue the legacy that her grandmother (Catherine Clark the 4th) and mother (Catherine Clark the 5th) passed down to her. She hopes to make a positive impact on children and families as they immerse themselves in her stories.

Visit www.CatherineClarkFelts.com to discover more books by the author.